G000155324

*Greater Than a
available in Eboo

Greater Than a Tourist Book Series
Reviews from Readers

I think the series is wonderful and beneficial for tourists to get information before visiting the city.

-Seckin Zumbul, Izmir Turkey

I am a world traveler who has read many trip guides but this one really made a difference for me. I would call it a heartfelt creation of a local guide expert instead of just a guide.

-Susy, Isla Holbox, Mexico

New to the area like me, this is a must have!

 -Joe, Bloomington, USA

This is a good series that gets down to it when looking for things to do at your destination without having to read a novel for just a few ideas.

-Rachel, Monterey, USA

Good information to have to plan my trip to this destination.

-Pennie Farrell, Mexico

Great ideas for a port day.

-Mary Martin USA

Aptly titled, you won't just be a tourist after reading this book. You'll be greater than a tourist!

-Alan Warner, Grand Rapids, USA

Even though I only have three days to spend in San Miguel in an upcoming visit, I will use the author's suggestions to guide some of my time there. An easy read - with chapters named to guide me in directions I want to go.

-Robert Catapano, USA

Great insights from a local perspective! Useful information and a very good value!

-Sarah, USA

This series provides an in-depth experience through the eyes of a local. Reading these series will help you to travel the city in with confidence and it'll make your journey a unique one.

-Andrew Teoh, Ipoh, Malaysia

GREATER THAN A TOURIST- NEW YORK USA

50 Travel Tips from a Local

Christina Fanelli

Greater Than a Tourist-New York State   Copyright © 2020 by CZYK Publishing LLC. All Rights Reserved.

All rights reserved. No part of this book may be reproduced in any form or by any electronic or mechanical means including information storage and retrieval systems, without permission in writing from the author. The only exception is by a reviewer, who may quote short excerpts in a review.

The statements in this book are of the authors and may not be the views of CZYK Publishing or Greater Than a Tourist.

First Edition

Cover designed by: Ivana Stamenkovic

Cover Image: https://pixabay.com/photos/architecture-new-york-city-manhattan-1850129/

Image 1: https://commons.wikimedia.org/wiki/File:Statue_of_Liberty,_NY.jpg William Warby / CC BY (https://creativecommons.org/licenses/by/2.0)

Image 2: https://commons.wikimedia.org/wiki/File:Lower_Manhattan_skyline_-_June_2017.jpg MusikAnimal / CC BY-SA (https://creativecommons.org/licenses/by-sa/4.0)

Image 3: https://commons.wikimedia.org/wiki/File:BuffaloSkyline.jpg Stephen Zimmermann / Public domain

Image 4: https://commons.wikimedia.org/wiki/File:Rochester_picture.jpg FBI / Public domain

CZYK Publishing Since 2011.
Greater Than a Tourist

Lock Haven, PA
All rights reserved.

ISBN: 9798656393898

>TOURIST

50 TRAVEL TIPS FROM A LOCAL

BOOK DESCRIPTION

With travel tips and culture in our guidebooks written by a local, it is never too late to visit New York. Greater Than a Tourist- New York State, USA by Author Christina Fanelli offers the inside scoop on The Empire State. Most travel books tell you how to travel like a tourist. Although there is nothing wrong with that, as part of the 'Greater Than a Tourist' series, this book will give you candid travel tips from someone who has lived at your next travel destination. This guide book will not tell you exact addresses or store hours but instead gives you knowledge that you may not find in other smaller print travel books. Experience cultural, culinary delights, and attractions with the guidance of a Local. Slow down and get to know the people with this invaluable guide. By the time you finish this book, you will be eager and prepared to discover new activities at your next travel destination.

Inside this travel guide book you will find:

Visitor information from a Local
Tour ideas and inspiration
Save time with valuable guidebook information

Greater Than a Tourist- A Travel Guidebook with 50 Travel Tips from a Local. Slow down, stay in one place, and get to know the people and culture. By the time you finish this book, you will be eager and prepared to travel to your next destination.

OUR STORY

Traveling is a passion of the Greater than a Tourist book series creator. Lisa studied abroad in college, and for their honeymoon Lisa and her husband toured Europe. During her travels to Malta, an older man tried to give her some advice based on his own experience living on the island since he was a young boy. She was not sure if she should talk to the stranger but was interested in his advice. When traveling to some places she was wary to talk to locals because she was afraid that they weren't being genuine. Through her travels, Lisa learned how much locals had to share with tourists. Lisa created the Greater Than a Tourist book series to help connect people with locals. A topic that locals are very passionate about sharing.

TABLE OF CONTENTS

BOOK DESCRIPTION

OUR STORY

TABLE OF CONTENTS

DEDICATION

ABOUT THE AUTHOR

HOW TO USE THIS BOOK

FROM THE PUBLISHER

WELCOME TO > TOURIST

1. Albany

2. Adirondacks

3. Adirondack Parks and Recreation

4. Saratoga

5. Lake Luzerne

6. Hadley

7. Gore Mountain

8. Ausable Chasm

9. Schuylerville

10.   Catskills

11.   Catskills Cycling

12.   Chautauqua

13.   Chautauqua Parks and Recreation

14.   Chautauqua History

15.   Chautauqua Entertainment

16.   Chautauqua Institution

17. Clymer

18. Clymer Entertainment

19. Ellicottville

20. Ellicottville Entertainment

21. Allegany Mountain

22. Lake Erie

23. Lake Erie Parks and Recreation

24. Lake Erie State Park and Ottoway Park

25. Lake Erie Entertainment

26.   Buffalo

27. Buffalo History and Entertainment

28. Cooperstown

29. Cooperstown Art and Entertainment

30.   Binghamton

31. Binghamton Entertainment

32. Binghamton Parks and Recreation

33. Binghamton Museums and History

34. Utica

35. Utica Entertainment

36. Union History

37. Utica Parks and Recreation

38. Rome

39. Rome History

40. Rome Parks and Recreation

41. Finger Lakes

42. Watkins Glen

43.   Watkins Glen Entertainment
44.   Watkins Glen Parks
45.   Watkins Glen History
46.   Rochester
47.   Rochester Entertainment
48.   Rochester Parks and Recreation
49.   Elmira
50.   Elmira Parks and Recreation

BONUS TIP 1.   Elmira History
BONUS TIP 2.   Corning
BONUS TIP 3.   Corning Entertainment
BONUS TIP 4.   Corning History
BONUS TIP 5.   Waterloo
BONUS TIP 6.   Syracuse
BONUS TIP 7.   Syracuse Entertainment
BONUS TIP 8.   Syracuse History
BONUS TIP 9.   Penn Yan
BONUS TIP 10.   Penn Yan Entertainment
BONUS TIP 11.   Letchworth Gorge
BONUS TIP 12.   Niagara Falls State Park
BONUS TIP 13.   Hudson Valley
BONUS TIP 14.   Hudson Valley Parks and Recreation
BONUS TIP 15.   Hudson Valley History
BONUS TIP 16.   Hudson Valley Entertainment

BONUS TIP 17.   Thousand Islands Seaway

BONUS TIP 18.   Thousand Islands Seaway History

BONUS TIP 19.   Thousand Islands Seaway Parks
and Recreation

BONUS TIP 20.   Long Island

BONUS TIP 21.   Long Island Entertainment

BONUS TIP 22.   Long Island Parks and Recreation

BONUS TIP 23.   Long Island History

BONUS TIP 24.   New York City

BONUS TIP 25.   New York City Entertainment

BONUS TIP 26.   New York City History

TOP REASONS TO BOOK THIS TRIP

References:

Packing and Planning Tips

Travel Questions

Travel Bucket List

NOTES

DEDICATION

To my kids, Miranda and William Green III for being who they really are and growing into such great adults and to Scott Congdon for giving the support to believe I could.

ABOUT THE AUTHOR

My name is Christina Fanelli, I live in Elmira, New York and I love to learn. I have lived here all my life and brought up my children in this area. Elmira has all of the seasons to celebrate and many places within it and nearby to travel for exciting experiences.

HOW TO USE THIS BOOK

The *Greater Than a Tourist* book series was written by someone who has lived in an area for over three months. The goal of this book is to help travelers either dream or experience different locations by providing opinions from a local. The author has made suggestions based on their own experiences. Please check before traveling to the area in case the suggested places are unavailable.

Travel Advisories: As a first step in planning any trip abroad, check the Travel Advisories for your intended destination.
https://travel.state.gov/content/travel/en/traveladvisories/traveladvisories.html

FROM THE PUBLISHER

Traveling can be one of the most important parts of a person's life. The anticipation and memories that you have are some of the best. As a publisher of the Greater Than a Tourist, as well as the popular *50 Things to Know* book series, we strive to help you learn about new places, spark your imagination, and inspire you. Wherever you are and whatever you do I wish you safe, fun, and inspiring travel.

Lisa Rusczyk Ed. D.
CZYK Publishing

WELCOME TO
> TOURIST

The Statue of Liberty in New York Harbor is a symbol of the United States and its ideals.

Lower Manhattan skyline as seen from Governors Island in June 2017.

Picture of Buffalo's downtown region taken from a hotel at sunset.

Rochester

"Make your mark in New York
and you are a made man."

– Mark Twain

B ack in 1624 along the Hudson River, a
colony was established by the Dutch called
New Amsterdam. It was on Manhattan
Island and became known as New York in 1664. It
was one of the first of the original 13 colonies that
made the American Revolution such a crucial
political role. Ellis Island has been estimated to have
been the pass through of about 40% of the millions of
American immigrants that arrived through the New
York Harbor between 1892 and 1954.

There are a lot of interesting facts that many
people do not know about New York State.

New York City was actually a capital of New
York back when the constitution was ratified in 1788.

Our first President, George Washington, was
inaugurated at the Federal Hall on Wall Street

The New York Evening Post was a federal
newspaper by Alexander Hamilton is now known as
the New York Post.

France gave The Statue of Liberty to the United
States as a gift supporting democracy and freedom.

Standing in the New York Harbor it welcomed over 14 million immigrants until 1924.

"Three Days of Peace and Music" was held by a dairy farmer on his land for the Woodstock Music Festival that had more than 400,000 in attendance.

Subway tracks 180 feet below the streets connect 468 subway stations and about 660 miles of track that more than 1.6 billion people rode just in one year.

There is over 6 million acres of protected land in the Adirondack Park in New York State. This is larger than well-known parks such as Yellowstone and Grand Canyon National Park combined.

Cooperstown New York contains the National Baseball Hall of Fame.

New York State is located in the North East of the United States. This makes for all of the season to be in full show, with beauty. "Make your mark" activities include in winter the mountains are covered snow; in the spring the open farm land starts to bud; oceans, lakes, and rivers come to life in the summer; and the beautiful trees show the most amazing colors come autumn. When people hear the State of New York, most of the people think New York City. There are some people that may think of Syracuse, Rochester, Buffalo, or even Binghamton and Jamestown, but nobody thinks of the smaller areas

and the different locations of entertainment,
sightseeing, and history.

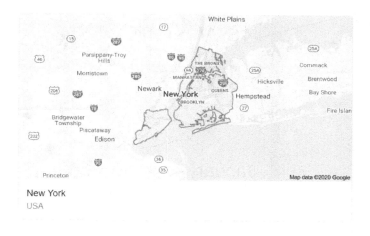

New York
USA

New York Climate

	High	Low
January	39	26
February	43	29
March	52	36
April	64	45
May	72	54
June	80	64
July	84	69
August	84	69
September	76	61
October	64	50
November	55	42
December	44	31

GreaterThanaTourist.com

Temperatures are in Fahrenheit degrees.
Source: NOAA

1. ALBANY

This being the state capital is well known. It has a bird museum with historic fire engines and some of the 9/11 World Trade Center remains. It is also known for the numerous breweries and the rums and whiskeys that started at the Albany Distilling Company back at the end of the 19th century.

Apex Entertainment Albany has Hologate, candlepin, simulated sports, and more. There is an indoor Rockgym for those that love rock climbing. There are half mile tunnels and a zip line that is 60-foot. Have you ever heard of Rugby? Check out the Albany Knickerbockers Rugby Club that has three men's sides and a Women's division one team all based from Dick Green Field in Albany. Albany Dutchmen is a baseball team that is part of Perfect Game Collegiate Baseball League. It runs early June through early August.

2. ADIRONDACKS

This natural area covers over six million acres with over 100 communities, mountains, valleys, cliffs and lakes. The Adirondacks have peaks that are used for anything from hiking to skiing. There are 12 regions, with lakeside resorts and campgrounds for bobsledding, winter safari, villages and forts, lakes contain beaches, cruises, and railroads to explore.

3. ADIRONDACK PARKS AND RECREATION

Adirondack Tug Hill – Most known for Off Highway Vehicle (OHV) riding such as dirt bikes, ATV's and UTV's on the recreation trails.

Adirondack Coast – There are museums that have histories about wars, railroads, and popular people like Samuel de Champlain and Alice T. Miner.

Malone Region is known for the annual Hatch Fly Fishing Tournament on Salmon River.

Adirondack Seaway is known as the World's Fishing Capital.

Adirondacks Hamilton County is known because it had the first hotel in the nation to have electricity on Blue Mount Lake.

Lake George Region has Six Flags Great Escape & Hurricane Harbor

Lake Placid Region holds the Summit Classic Lacrosse, Marathon/Half Marathon, and Can-Am Rugby Tournament.

Whiteface Region has gorges that are attractive to hikers and mountain bikers.

Saranac Lake Region has great mountain biking and fat biking trails.

Lake Champlain Region known for its Champlain Area Trails (CATS) paths to explore the Ausable Chasm.

Tupper Lake Region has the Tuber Lake Triad hiking challenge that takes hikers to a fire tower peak.

Schroon Lake Region has an annual ADK Unite run.

4. SARATOGA

Saratoga is known for its publication in Sports Illustrated because it has the Saratoga Race track that is known as the oldest sporting venue and rated among the top 10. There are even Ghost Tours! There is Saratoga Paint and Sip Studio – Enjoy a cocktail while you watch an artist instruct you through a piece of art and in the end take home a painting that shows beautiful art. Have you ever tried Tango dancing? Private lessons are available for adults and children with other styles of dance such as Salsa, Swing, Foxtrot, Waltz and partner dancing. There are many different forms of art all the way from Frances Young Tang Teaching Museum and Art Gallery to Skidmore College. There is bowling, bumper cars, arcade games that have redemption and End Zone Sports pubs. EnLiven Retreats, LLC offers classes for your body including Yoga, Zumpa, massages, mineral baths, and more.

Want to break the summer heat, come to Adirondack Adventure Center for Tubing and Rafting Adventures and for lazy river tubing and rafting the whitewater. It is close to Lake George in Lake Luzerne, New York.

Another water park, Six Flags Great Escape Lodge & Indoor Waterpark, is also near Lake George in Queensbury, New York. It also has 200 suites that are available. There is also an Adventure Family Fun Center that contains, Arcade Bumper Cars, Go Karts, Paintball, Laser Tag and more.

Do you want to break they kids of the technology world? Bring them to an old-fashioned farm full of activities at Ellms Family Farm in Ballston Spa, New York. It includes pumpkin picking, corn mazes and more.

5. LAKE LUZERNE

Lake Luzerne, New York as ADK Treetop adventures through the forest canopy. Ride zip lines and wooden platforms and a state-of-the-art adventure course.

6. HADLEY

Hadley, New York is also near Lake George. The Hudson and Sacandaga Rivers come together for the best rafting, tubing, and kayaking all located in the Sacandaga Outer Center.

7. GORE MOUNTAIN

Gore Mountain is in North Creek, New York with an upstate premier family oriented ski resort. There is dining and 110 trails that cover 2,527 vertical feet!

8. AUSABLE CHASM

Ausable Chasm, New York is compared to the Grand Canyon. It is up to five miles of trails for raft trips, rock climbing, and scenic walking and hiking.

9. SCHUYLERVILLE

Schuylerville, NY has Olde Saratoga Farms. It is known for riding lessons, hormanship, and chiropractics.

10. CATSKILLS

If you love the outdoors, the beauty and adventure that you will find in the Catskills are just for you. There are Thomas Cole's 19th century paintings, lessons in fly-tying, shrine and art collections, and museums of music, and art from the 1960s. There are biking resorts with miles of a high-speed quad lifts and water parks, casinos, and raceway.

There are scenic drives and bridges that are covered on the way through 20th century landmarks. Take this trip and get a chance to see the Woodstock makings, Shawangunk Mountains, Neversink River, all the way to the scene that inspired Rip Van Winkle.

Have you ever tried fly fishing? Some of the best known waterways for fly fishing are right here and visited by well-known Theodore Gordon, the 'Father of American Dry Fly Fishing.'. These areas include:

the Town of Roscoe, Delaware River, Neversink River, The Esopus Creek, and Batavia Kill.

There are lakes, ponds, creeks, streams, and more that are perfect for swimming, a canoe, rowboat, kayak or whatever other paddling craft you have.

Here are some of the best spots in the Catskills to plan for paddling: The Delaware River, Alder Lake, Batavia Kill, North-South Lake, and Hanes Falls to Mongaup Pond. Each of these has their own eye catcher such as the oldest fire tower, to the best fishing holes.

11. CATSKILLS CYCLING

If you are one of the many that love to go bicycling Catskills has the trails for you. There are trails for newbies to enhance your skills on the beginner trails all the way to the gravel roads for intermediate terrain. During these rides see the dairy farms and farmer's markets. Some of the trails are called loops ranging from 12 to 73 miles and easy to difficult based on the elevation, they are:

- Cherry Ridge
- Wild Forest Loop
- Moticello Loop
- Short Tour of the Shawangunks

- Grand Fondo Tour.

There is also cycling events through-out the year, but the well-known ones are they tour of the Catskills that is held every year in the summer and the Women's Woodstock cycling Grand Prix this is traveling of over 50 miles.

If you enjoy motorcycle rides, here are some rallies and festivals to check out: The Catskill Mountain Thunder Motorcycle Rally in East Durham. Colors in the Catskills at Hunter Mountain. Spring Run at Blackthorne Resort.

There are also popular routes for motorcycles through scenic counties on different routes that will visit the eight best breweries, ice cream spots, small towns, and cideries.

12. CHAUTAUQUA

Known for mountains, lakes, and vineyards, this area also has playgrounds, beaches, trails, bridle paths, and boating sites near camp grounds and cabins. There is an amusement park that is over 100 years old with fishing and docks. If history is on the itinerary, Chautauqua has 12 museums.

13. CHAUTAUQUA PARKS AND RECREATION

Dunkirk Lighthouse Park and Veterans Museum – has a 61 foot tower with military and maritime artifacts.

Grape Discovery Center Wine! Well and grape juice too. Both are available for tasting, with cheeses, cured meats, while enjoying Arts & Crafts, Glasses & Mugs, and more.

Lawson Boating Heritage Center A great site for boating history, fun displays and special events like private parties.

Midway State Park is one of the oldest operating amusement parks that originated in 1898 as a trolley park.

14. CHAUTAUQUA HISTORY

Fenton History Center A mansion of exhibits of local history and a library of reference/genealogy.

Lily Dale Assembly Museum The birth of Spiritualism and its history at this landmark.

Lucy Desi Museum For arts iconic speakers, performers, and comedy the Lucille Ball Desi Arnaz Museum & Comedy Center in Jamestown

McClurg Museum It a 14 room Federal style mansion built in 1883. There are salons and formal rooms.

Robert H. Jackson Center a liberty library of the life and work of Supreme Court Justice Robert H. Jackson and issues and events. There is a 200 seat theater, banquet reception, and conference rooms.

Roger Tory Peterson Institute of Natural History a spectacular exhibit of 27 acres wood setting hiking trails and nature art exhibitions.

Yorker Museum has the old setting of the general store, schoolhouse, buggy shed, chapel and more.

15. CHAUTAUQUA ENTERTAINMENT

National Comedy Center Come visit this center also named as one of the "World's Greatest Places" by Time and by People as "100 Reasons to Love America". It will inspire, education, and entertain.

16. CHAUTAUQUA INSTITUTION

Chautauqua Institution has different kinds of entertainment available year round. Visit here to see there different world-class artists, preachers, and speaker. They have different types of sporting events to try such as golf, tennis, and water sports such as sailing and fishing. In the summer there is a nine-week artistic educational, interfaith, and recreational program in session.

There are bus trips available with a guide and plenty of exhibits, performances, lectures, readings and classes to visit along with the Heirloom Restaurant in the historic lakefront Athenaeum Hotel.

17. CLYMER

Clymer is named after George Clymer, a Declaration of Independence signer. This area has different types of entertainment, some for those that like golf in more than one location with more than just golf to offer.

18. CLYMER ENTERTAINMENT

Aerial Adventure Course There are golf courses, Giant Zip lines, soaring Eagle, biking, indoor and outdoor pools, and spas.

Peek'n Peak Resort is known for PGA Tours, Korn Ferry Tour, and stunning views. The golf tees cover over 7,000 yards! There is a Pool and Play Zone that has a lifeguard and hot tub. Weddings & Meetings can be held with a variety of accommodations, leisure and luxury amenities.

Serenity Spa has the treatment of the body and mind. Anything from Hot Stone Massage to facials and Botanical Skin Resurfacing.

19. ELLICOTTVILLE

Ellicottville is known as the New York playground for the outside. It has different kinds of entertainment for fun and adventure with the 20 shops, restaurants, bars and 2 ski slopes that are all within walking distance.

It is known for the mountain bike trails, Spruce Lake kayaking, and Mountain Coaster Park and Sky High Adventure Park. There are bed and breakfasts available after a couples night life and hotels and condos for families.

20. ELLICOTTVILLE ENTERTAINMENT

In July there is a summer Music Festival that is held by the Chamber of Commerce and an Ellicottville Gazebo series that is sponsored by the CCSE Federal Credit Union that also has different kinds of bands and excitement.

21. ALLEGANY MOUNTAIN

Allegany Mountain resort is a camping and Cabin site that is nearby that has different types of entertainment within for families. There is an indoor and an outdoor pool, and playgrounds, along with woods to hike.

22. LAKE ERIE

Bordering New York, Pennsylvania, Michigan, Ohio and Ontario Canada Lake Erie is the fourth largest Great Lake. The shoreline is almost 10,000 square miles and the average depth is 62 feet deep.

One person rafts are available at Solo Duckie tours and Zoar Valley Rafting.

Panama Rocks Park has great hikes among the rock formations and nature to the Griffis Sculpture Park.

23. LAKE ERIE PARKS AND RECREATION

La Salle Park, Buffalo will be coming to life in New York at the mouth of the Niagara River. It will be featuring fields for concerts, picnics, playing, dogs, and more. Be sure to watch for this opening!

Erin Basin Marina and Gardens is a waterfront park that has a full service marine at the mouth of the Buffalo River. There is a tower that has fabulous views of the waterfront and of Buffalo with ice cream, restaurants art displays, and gardens to also be enjoyed.

Are you into observing our service members? Come to the Veterans Park and the navel and Military Park by Lake Erie on the Buffalo River side. It has a museum of vessels, a cruiser, submarine, and a destroyer. On the US coast Guard property, there is a Lighthouse from 1833 that is now accessible for public tours.

If water is something of an interest, check out the Times Beach Nature Preserve and the Wilkeson Pointe Park. These are areas that are full of history such as a recovered waste disposal site that now has great hiking trails, bird watching sites, and beautiful landscaping and beaches.

Greenway Nature Trail and Outer Harbor have large concert venue and the some of the enations larges bands.

NFTA Boat harbor Park and Gallagher Beach is a marina with over 1000 boats and ships and it is open the public. There are stores, restaurants, and piers with gorgeous views.

Woodlawn Beach State Park on Lake Erie and operated by the Town of Hamburg. There is a swimming beach, restaurant, nature center, trails, kids' area for play, and snacks. There is also the Hamburg Town Clock that is a small viewing area with lake-side diners and the Hamburg Beach Park, that has a sandy swimming beach, changing rooms, snack bar, and a fitness center that can be visited with a resident permit.

Lake Erie Seaway Trial Visitor Center has a must come and see areas. It has some of the most breathtaking views of the Lake Erie sunsets while learning about western Seaway Trail history, culture, environment, and view the scenic, recreational sources.

Wendt Beach Park and Sturgeon Point Marina are some have to sees. Sturgeon Point and Wendt Beach Park have boat launches, dry docks, snack shops, picnic areas, slips, playing fields, nature trails, and beautiful views.

Bennett Beach Park and Lake Erie Beach Park are large swimming beach areas with sand dunes, playgrounds, picnic areas, basketball courts and fishing.

Evans Town Park, George Borello Park and Evangola State Park are community parks to visit. They have playing fields for sports, playgrounds, lakefront parks, picnic areas along the beach, nature trials, pavilions for parties, wildlife and campgrounds.

Cattaraugus Creek Boat Launch and Town Hanover Beach and Silver Creek Rest Area have DEC boat launches, piers, guarded swimming areas, picnic tables, pavilions, and playgrounds.

Sheridan Bay Park and Wright Park are both along the lake and have sandy beaches, campgrounds, shelters, and different types of sports features such as ball fiends and basketball courts.

City of Dunkirk has a Memorial Park to honor the city's Veterans, a navigational beacon build in 1875 on Gratiot Point with a beacon that still operates. There is a park with a beach, picnic facility, playgrounds, sandy swimming beach and a ball-field.

24. LAKE ERIE STATE PARK AND OTTOWAY PARK

Lake Erie State Park and Ottoway Park are campgrounds with pavilions, walking paths, hiking trails, picnic facilities and scenic beaches.

25. LAKE ERIE ENTERTAINMENT

Barcelona Harbor and Lighthouse with a lake access parking lot makes for a great place to view Lake Erie, fish, and see the 1828 Barcelona Lighthouse.

To view 23 wineries visit the Lake Erie Wine Country. The Southern Tier has award winning brewing companies and Amish Trails to shop for hand-crafts.

26. BUFFALO

Buffalo now has a redeveloped waterfront that is surrounded by neighborhoods that have been revitalized. Buffalo is known for its different types of excitement. There is anything from entrepreneurs to artists each with a story and a place to visit to see it for you yourself and learn while having fun.

Have you ever heard of Buffalo wings? Where do you think that started? Right here! Anchor Bar invented Buffalo-style chicken wings back in 1964. Since that time the history and character is known in 13 of the pubs in the eater's guide to the tastiest.

What is the most popular answer to what is the best drink with chicken wings? Beer! In 1919, just before the Prohibition, Buffalo had 29 breweries and over 8,000 establishments to enjoy it in. Today there are 35 breweries and five distilleries

27. BUFFALO HISTORY AND ENTERTAINMENT

Visit areas where history was made, by where President Theodore Roosevelt took oath, or just relax at the Canalside or Larkin Square. Would you like to see Niagara Falls, come to Buffalo. Canalside hosts events all year to the public. These events range from festivals, to fitness classes and ice skating.

If you have an interest in Architecture Buffalo is a place to visit. There are landmarks from Frank Lloyd Wright's Martin House Complex to the skyscraper of Guaranty Building. There are Eliel and Eero Saarinen's Kleinhans Music Hall and Elbert Hubbard's Roycroft Campus. These are structures that are breathtaking and priceless memories.

If you would like a night out on the town, Buffalo has plenty for you to choose from. There are sites that have stand-up comedians while enjoying a beer and live music. There is gambling in casinos with dinners and drinks. Would you like to see performing arts go to the Buffalo After Dark or Nightlife.

There are plenty of activities to do outside in Buffalo. Try city tours and garden walks. How about fishing hot spots, golf courses or sailing on a Great Lake. Is it winter time? Try ice biking or skiing.

Of course don't forget the good old Buffalo Bills Football team. Or maybe some NHL Sabres, NLL Bandits, Women's Beauts pro hockey, Queen City Roller Girls and the AAA baseball Bisons. Want sports, we have them covered.

With all this exciting entertainment there is, of course, the best lodging available. Roycroft Inn is great for history fanatics because it is a National Historic Landmark. The Hotel @ the Lafayette or the Mansion on Delaware are for the architectural fanatics. However, if you would just like to be pampered, check out the Hyatt Regency, Marriott Harbor Center or the Embassy Suites.

There are various types of art throughout Buffalo. Buffalo Burchfield Penney Art Center (BPAC) has famous Charles Burchfield's watercolor art and they host happy hours and concerts.

- CEPA Photography art
- Big Orbit Gallery is contains innovative art
- Squeaky Wheel Film
- Media Art Center has films, video and media.
- Buffalo Art Studio has working arts to visitors can watch the art in the making.
- UB Anderson Gallery was established by New York Martha Jackson's son David Anderson and later

donated to the University of Buffalo has 1,200 works of art by noted modernist artists.

• On the campuses north end is UB Art Gallery are national artists

• Drive 30 minutes from Buffalo and you will find Castellani Museum on the Niagara University campus. It is a rational and national art collage that has work by Helen Frankenthaler, Georges Rouault, William DeKooning, Keith Haring, and Pablo Picasso on a rotation basis.

Buffalo has the well-known Philharmonic Orchestra, but how about the Asbury Hall@ Babeville or the Town Ballroom? Would you like some rock club grit at the Mohawk Place or maybe some country music at the Sportsmen's Tavern. Jazz is available at the Colored Musicians Club and Pausa Art House has something different with Nietzsche's bohemian just around the corner.

28. COOPERSTOWN

Cooperstown is known for its possession of The National Baseball Hall of Fame & Museum along with a beverage trail and Fenimore Art Museum.

However, there are events that happen throughout the year for different age groups.

How about a family harvesting and processing of wool? Come here and learn how to shear the sheep. Then learn how to do the sorting, washing, skirting and drying of the fleece that will come from the picking, teasing, combing and spinning for the wool into a yarn that you can take home.

29. COOPERSTOWN ART AND ENTERTAINMENT

Art is displayed from different known artists with a musical performance from a live jazz guitarist. Admission is free and visit productions form Pooh Kaye, Eileen Crowell, and Ruben and Damian Salinas. This means you will see art that ranges from film and media to drama and black tempera on paper.

If you have an interest in birds, come see the birds from near and far in a digital presentation. It is a presentation of photographs by award winning Gail and Nelson Dubois. You can also sign up for the DOAS Big Day. It is the Delaware-Otsego Audubon Society event to identify as many species of birds as possible during one day and help team members learn. Members learn about the area, birds, and get to travel the area.

30. BINGHAMTON

Binghamton is located in the center of Broome County with valleys through Susquehanna, Chenango, Tioughnioga and Otselic rivers. Otsego Lake converges with the Chenango River through to Pennsylvania with fresh water of more than 19 million galls a minute into Chesapeake Bay. Binghamton did cigar production in the 1800s, Endicott-Johnson Shoes, and the birth of computers with the home of Thomas J. Watson later known as Internationals Business Machines (IBM).

Spiedie sandwiches came over with the Italians in the 1920s, but also became one of Binghamton's most famous sandwiches. Check out the originality.

When it becomes autumn, check out the pumpkins! There is Jackson's Farm for picking pumpkins and the famous Iron Kettle Farm for the corn maze at Stoughton Farm.

31. BINGHAMTON ENTERTAINMENT

Robot City Games is located in Binghamton and is the biggest game center in New York State. It is known because of it still having some of the classic games like arcade games, Donkey Kong, Crazy Taxi and more.

Did you know that there was a Carousel Capital of the world? There is and it is right here, they were built back in the 1920s and are known as the Rec Park Carousel and the Highland Park Carousel.

Ice Hockey is a game that Binghamton strives on. Floyd L. Maines Veterans Memorial Arena has the Binghamton Senators Ice Hockey games, hot pretzels, churros, and more.

If you like Opera or have never tried it, here is one to try. Tri-Cities Opera is culturally enriched and educational and has been around since 1949.

32. BINGHAMTON PARKS AND RECREATION

Binghamton Zoo at Ross Park has animals from snow leopards and penguins to otter pups available for visitors to see. There are reduced rates for senior citizens, college students, military members, and children. Children under 2 are free.

A nationally recognized museum that is located in Binghamton is the Roberson Museum and Science center. They have sci-fi conventions, food fests, and art exhibitions all year.

33. BINGHAMTON MUSEUMS AND HISTORY

If you like antiques, check out the Phelps Mansion Museum. It dates back to 1870 and was constructed during the Victorian Period so it has the crystal chandeliers and beautiful wood.

Binghamton has history of the fully restored carousel from 1925 that inspired the "Walking Distance" episode of the Twilight Zone.

Kopernik Observatory & Science Center has great stargazing equipment for public observations.

If you like Cider, check out the 1926 landmark Cider Mill that has baked goods, fruit wine, and of course, apple cider.

34. UTICA

Utica has what is called Bagg's Square, a long lost hotel that was known to have had guests such as George Washington and Ulysses S. Grant. These famous names along with the Utica Children's Museum make it a landmark area in New York state.

There is a hotel in Utica that has the old fashioned architectural charms that caught the eyes of guests such as Judy Garland and President Roosevelt.

There are bike trails that follow the Eric Canal and ride for almost 36 miles.

35. UTICA ENTERTAINMENT

Utica Marina is a historical building on the waterway that hold banquets in the two story structure that has both restaurant and patio seating.

Want to visit a zoo. Check out the Utica Zoo. It is more than 40 acres and has almost 100 different species. It is a children oriented zoo with anything from alligators to zebras.

Do you know any of the names Goo Goo Dolls, REO Speedwagon, or Tony Bennett? These are all concerts that have performed at the Baroque-style Stanley Theatre. Stop by and check out the Theatre!

Utica Children's Museum has exhibits that will tag a "natural curiosity" in a child. These range from hands on exhibits to wooden trains sets and space exploration exhibits.

If you would just like to relax? Check out Pixley Park for family and friends entertainment with sports courts and playgrounds and Chancellor Park for a good leisurely stroll.

Golf of 18 holes is available at the Valley View Golf Course. It has been around for almost a century and has water features, tree lines holes, and chipping and putting practice facilities. When done playing, there is a Valley View Café with sandwiches and beverages or a bar in Daniels that has Italian dishes.

Try a Lava Spa or just get a little relaxation. Massage and spa treatments are available to refresh and rejuvenate. There waxing and nails care treatments along with mud puddles for feet and for the neck, head and shoulders, try hot oils.

36. UNION HISTORY

Union Station is from the day of marble-style columns, vaulted ceilings and cathedral transport. It brings the aura to the railway station and that still functions.

37. UTICA PARKS AND RECREATION

The Mohawk River helps preserve the Utica Marsh Wildlife Management area wet meadows and marsh. Birdwatchers and natures fans must visit the trains and boardwalks to the two observation towers.

Proctor Park is actually two parks. FT and TR parks combined so that gives visitors floral displays to observe, four baseball fields, soccer pitches, running trails and basketball courts.

Munson-Williams-Proctor Arts Institute is an art institute that had some of the most famous figures like Andy Warhol, Jackson Pollock and Georgia O'Keeffe

FX Matt Brewing Company dates all the back to the 1800s. It was the first brewery to gain a license after the 1930s prohibition.

38. ROME

Rome is known as the Copper City because it produced about 10 percent of the United States Copper during the Industrial Revolution. Now it focuses on cybersecurity initiatives, (UAS) Unmanned Aerial Systems working with different

world known areas such as the (AFRL) Air Force
Research Laboratory.

39. ROME HISTORY

If there is a history buff on the trip, check out the
Sears Oil Co. Museum that was a historical gas
station with the old fashioned pumps and the Rome
Historical Society & Museum that has the French and
Indian War Fortification, Tomb of the unknown, and
the Lower Landing site.

Rome Sports Hall of Fame is a non-profit
organization with over 50 exhibits. It has photos,
uniforms, gear and uniforms of victorious moments in
sports.

Fort Stanwix National Monument and Marinus
Willett Center was built during the French and Indian
War to protect the Onieda Carry. It was used to
shield the American troops during the siege in 1777
and was successful. There are stories and exhibits
inside the state-of-the-art facility.

40. ROME PARKS AND RECREATION

Bellamy Harbor Park is known for kayaking. The Park has a launch for canoes and kayaks for fishing and Fort Stanwix is a great place for picnicking, boating, and hosting events.

A film festival with live theatrical performances, dance programs, and silent plays can be seen at the Capitol Theater.

Everyone knows who JFK was, but the J. F. Kennedy Arena is an ice hockey academy for the Varsity Hockey Team, but it also has events and figure skating.

If skiing is on the itinerary, check out the Woods Valley Ski Area. There are slopes for beginners to expert skiers. There is snow tubing areas, good lighting for night skiers, and a rental shop.

If you like fall foliage and wildlife, check out the Griffiss International Sculpture Garden. There are designs from famous artist, modern art sculptures.

What used to be a sand mining pit is now a hiking trail. It is .7 miles long Sand Dune Trail of old wood roads and paths that were used for logging.

Fort Rickey Children's Discovery Zoo not only has animals, but it has hands-on animal shows, a tunnel maze, and a giant tube for kids.

Artistree Studios & Gallery is for art lovers. It is a non-profit organization that has kids, teenagers, and adults in mind.

Delta Lake State Park has camping sites for tents, trailers, and RV's. It is by the lake so you can enjoy the scenery.

41. FINGER LAKES

One of the most beautiful regions is the eleven finger-shaped lakes in the heart of New York. There are numerous different areas in the Finger Lakes that have beautiful places to visit with a lot of excitement to boot.

42. WATKINS GLEN

Watkins Glen is a small village that has the vineyards and wineries along the Seneca Lake, but there a different place to visit.

43. WATKINS GLEN
ENTERTAINMENT

The Watkins Glen International Race track is at that southern end of Seneca Lake. The have held races yearly for 20 years. These races include Grand Prix, NASCAR, IndyCar Series, Can-Am, Trans-Am and more! Finger Lakes Wine Festival is a three-day event that is held every July at the Watkins Glen International Race Track. There are different showcases along with vendors of wines, musical instruments, live music and food.

Captain Bill's Seneca Lake Cruises provide an hour cruise to view the lake and enjoy a dinner, lunch, or cocktails in the afternoon.

Farm Sanctuary has rescued over 500 animals that range from pigs, turkeys, cows and more. They spread out over 271 acres of scenic land. There are guides that will tell the stories of the different animals that are now happy in the natural environment.

44. WATKINS GLEN PARKS

Hector Falls is a waterfall that runs along Route 414. Rent a boat and see the falls cascade into massive falls after passing over limestone. These falls are 165 feet high, but some summers are so dry, they are just a trickle.

There is also a New York State Park in Watkins Glen. It contains the Rainbow Falls and a stream that drops 400 feet past 200 foot cliffs that make falls like you can only imagine. There is a Gorge Trail that can be hiked and a stone bridge to cross over the water.

Take the Seneca Lake Wine Trail to try 35 different wineries. These wines include chardonnay, Riesling, cabernet franc, and pinot noir for hard to find native grapes.

Watkins Glen also has a State Park that has streams that are 2-miles long, 400 feet drops, 200-foot cliffs and trails through the gorge that walk right under the waterfalls! There is a pool open in the summer and picnic areas and campsites.

45. WATKINS GLEN HISTORY

Brick Tavern Museum was built in 1828. It has displays of some of the Native American medical artifacts, textiles, transportation, and more.

In 1983 Castel Grisch was established on 150 acres to grow the best grapes to make the best wine. There is a tasting room and they have small meals for lunches and an indoor or an outdoor seating for the best views.

46. ROCHESTER

Rochester is known for the lilacs, theater, and being near Lake Ontario and all the entertainment these bring parts of nature bring.

Lilacs are so popular in Rochester that they have an annual festival. At these festivals there are popular drinks such as wine from Lilac Hill Wine Vineyard and Black Button Lilac Gin that can be purchased while walking all 150 acres of Highland Park.

47. ROCHESTER ENTERTAINMENT

For kids entertainment there is the Limitless Coloring Page and Educational Scavenger Hunts. These hunts explore most school topics like History, Math, Geography, Art, etc. or stick to the Sciences of Earth, Biology, Astronomy, and more.

Want family entertainment, Rochester has theatres, museums, and science centers along with landmarks for adults and Strong National Museum of Play and Seabreeze Amusement Park for the family.

48. ROCHESTER PARKS AND RECREATION

Want to be outside in the sunshine and walk or hike? There are 21 parks in Monroe County and the City of Rochester offers recreation a many of the parks.

Along the Erie Canal running and biking can be done on the canal path with starting points in seven different towns.

There are golf courses in Durand Eastman, Genesee Valley, and Churchville if you would like to play for the day or just at each.

There is Maple Sugar Season in Rochester to enjoy the warm days and chilly nights as the Maple Trees flow the sugar! Come sample our famous maple sugar candy.

49. ELMIRA

Elmira is a city that is located just above the Pennsylvania borderline. It is the most well-known because of being the home of the Author, Mark Twain

50. ELMIRA PARKS AND RECREATION

Dunn Field is a baseball stadium that was built on November 31, 1902. It can seat up to 4,020 and the dimensions of right field and left lines are 325 feet, and 386 feet to straightaway center field. It has had different baseball legends that have played there such as "Hall of Famers Earl Weaver and Wade Boggs, legendary manager Lou Piniella, current Washington Nationals manager Davey Johnson, current Tampa Bay Rays bench coach Don Zimmer, and two-time World Series Champion, Curt Schilling." (Elmira College, Dunn Field, 2020)

Harris Hill is a park that was established in 1947 for family entertainment. They have pay-as-you-go games and food, rides, and picnic areas. There are batting cages, miniature golf and driving rages, go carts, sailplane rides, and the National Soaring Museum and Tanglewood Nature Center.

Eldridge Park opened on July 4, 1926. It covers about 15 acres of land and his known for its updates in the 1960's of "outdoor stage, an extensive network of picnic areas, a wooden roller coaster, haunted house, shooting gallery bumper cars, rides for young and old alike, Jasper II (a boat ride on the park's lake), eateries, a miniature golf course, and a small-gauge train that ran through the park, in addition to several other rides and attractions." It has one of the few remaining 18 carousels in the US that still has a brass ring feeder. It also has soccer fields, a skate park, and a baseball field.

Chemung River Friends is approximately 500 years of Native American History available with Canoe or Kayak rentals.

First Arena was built back in 2004. It is the home of the Elmira Enforcers of the Federal Prospects Hockey in 2018. It has seasonal ice hockey games and other types of entertainment throughout the year.

BONUS TIP 1.   ELMIRA HISTORY

Famous People there are numerous Famous people from Elmira, such as Tommy Hilfiger. Fashion Designer. Beth Phoenix. Wrestler. Jeanine Pirro. Reality Star, Charlie Baker. Politician. Pilar Sanders. Reality Star. Jason Butler Harner. Tedd Arnold.

Young Adult Author. However, the most well know is Mark Twain. Mark Twain is most well-known for his stories of Tom Sawyer and Huckleberry Finn. He began his life in Elmira in 1867 and fell in love with Olivia Langdon who died in 1904 at 59 and that depression put an end to his writing; he died 6 years later. In Elmira is their home, grave sites, Mark Twain's Study, and exhibits.

Elmira College is a private college of liberal arts that is one of the oldest colleges still existing that grant women equivalent degrees as men. It was founded in 1855 with Victorian buildings and collegiate, gothic architectural styles. The school colors are purple and gold and they offer 35 major areas of study leading to either BS or BA degrees.

Lake Erie College of Osteopathic Medicine (LECOM) offers College of Osteopathic Medicine, School of Pharmacy, School of Dental Medicine, Masters Degree Programs, School of Health Services Administration, Pharmacy Post Baccalaureate Program and Pre-PharmD Enrichment Program. There are also Post Graduate programs for Physicians, Pharmacists, Continuing Medical Education PRIME Conference, and LECOMT OPTI/GME. It is a new building that has just recently finished construction.

Elmira Railroad was organized in in 1832, running to Williamsport PA. Northern Central Railway leased it in 1863, and in 190 Pennsylvania Railroad leased it until the flood of 1972.

BONUS TIP 2. CORNING

Corning is known as the Crystal City. It is a town dubbed "The Gaffer District". It is known for the Corning Museum of Glass art and glassblowing shots.

The Gaffer district has downtown streets of antique shops, galleries, and boutiques that can be visited while viewing the Centennial Park clock tower with dinner.

BONUS TIP 3. CORNING ENTERTAINMENT

Southern Tier Kayak Tours are available along the Chemung River between Corning and Elmira. Quick paddling lessons are available or take an expert guide. There is plenty of wildlife to see, maybe even a bald eagle!

There is the Chocolate trail for chocolate lovers. 30 establishments have cocoa items for you to experience. You will be able to get anything from dark chocolate balsamic vinegar to peanut butter chocolate ribbon pie.

Keuka Lake Wine Trail is famous for its Riesling. The area is also known for New York's Dr. Konstantin Frank award-winning winery.

BONUS TIP 4. CORNING HISTORY

Corning Museum of Glass gives a new outlook to visitors on glass and science. However, did you know the screen on your smartphone came from here? Spend hours learning about the last 35 centuries of glass history and watch experts do hot glass demonstrations or make your own glass vase, wind chime, eggs, and much, much more.

Rockwell Museum focuses on Native American art and shows the landscapes by Audubon. There are pings by Charles Russell and sculptures by Frederic Remington. Kids have I-Spy, make puppets, cardboard villages are available to play in, and draw a portrait.

BONUS TIP 5.   WATERLOO

Waterloo is known as the birthplace of Memorial Day based on Nelson Rockefeller proclaiming that Waterloo "first, formal, complete, well-planned, village-wide observance of a day entirely dedicated to honoring the war dead."

The First Presbyterian Church in 1851 was established in Waterloo, it is a beautiful site to see.

Tom Coughlin from the New York Giants has a large mural downtown. Mary Ann M'Clintock hosted the First Women's Rights Convention and her house is now owned by the National Park Service. The house is stationed on the Underground Railroad.

Oak Island has nature trails, fishing and picnic areas, boat launches and dock areas for entertainment on the Seneca-Cayuga canal.

If you like to shop checkout Waterloo's Premium Outlets, Destiny USA, and check out the Muranda Cheese Company.

There is also a cemetery of called the American Civil War Memorial. It has stones sent from 36 States. It has Men's and Women's Cenotaphs for those that served during the war.

BONUS TIP 6.   SYRACUSE

Syracuse has fun events all four seasons of the year. These events can be for adults, for kids, for families, and special events

BONUS TIP 7.   SYRACUSE ENTERTAINMENT

Armory Square and the Regal has a 60 foot IMAX Screen in the former Armory building with shopping dining and night events.

The Carrier Dome has more sports in mind. It is the home of the Syracuse University Orange NCAA Division I football, basketball, and lacrosse teams. Therefore, this domed stadium is great year round and seats 50,000.

Destiny USA has more than 200 retail venues of dining and entertainment. There is a full food court, carousel vintage, electric go-karts and savings programs for AAA/CAA cards.

Dinosaur BBQ is known around the world as the national favorite. It has been voted the Best Barbecue in American on "Good Morning America Weekend". There are different kinds of sauces to try along with funky wall art and different blues music for entertainment while you dine.

Animals have a home in Syracuse at the Rosamond Gifford Zoo at Burnet Park. There are over 700 animals that can be seen year round. These animals range from penguins and bears outdoors to lions and birds indoors.

Ever wonder why the stop light is on the top? So did the Irish. They decided it should be changed and put the green "Irish" on the top of the light and the red "British" on the bottom of the light. If you would like to see this "upside-down traffic light," come to Tipp Hill on Syracuse's West side.

BONUS TIP 8. SYRACUSE HISTORY

The Rock and Roll Hall of Fame and Museum in Cleveland and the local Everson were designed by I.M. Pei. There is a display of American ceramics, rotating exhibits of children's interactive gallery and a gift shop.

Erie Canal Museum was established in 1850 in the Weighlock Building. It has displays of treasured artifacts, maps, and replica of a canal boat with crew quarters, and cargo. Onondaga Historical Association

Museum and Research Center has regional collections of great size. It celebrates events, sport legends, industries, architecture, the Underground Railroad in Syracuse and more.

BONUS TIP 9.   PENN YAN

Penn Yan has shopping, vineyards, bulk foods, beautiful places to eat with great food.

Looking for unique or antique? The Windmill Farm & Craft Market has about 200 vendors and 30 years of operation. There is vintage cars, produce, furniture, and food made on the spot.

How about stocking up on supplies that you know that you will use, just maybe not right now. Come to the Oak Hill Bulk Foods and stock up on snacks and grocery store items and put them in the freezer. Try Amish Cheese imported from Pennsylvania. There is a deli in the store for bakery, deli, and café items to try.

BONUS TIP 10. PENN YAN ENTERTAINMENT

If you like wine, you will love Penn Yan. There are two well-known Vineyards, the Fox Run and Keuka Springs. Fox Run has tours of the vineyard. The wine making facility offers wine and cheese boards to get you hooked. Keuka Spring has a view of Keuka Lake that will take your breath away.

Have you ever tried Meadery? Mother Nature's nectar, Honey. Earle Estates Meader has what is commonly called "Honey Wine". They have proudly received Gold, Silver, and Bronze medals along with class awards.

When it comes time to eat check out Top of the Lake or the Keuka Restaurant. Both are great for families and have gorgeous views.

BONUS TIP 11. LETCHWORTH GORGE

Letchworth Gorge is also known as the "Grand Canyon of the East" in the eastern side of the United States. If you like the outdoors, here is your place to visit. They have hot air balloon rides, campsites, and water sports.

There are Major waterfalls among the cliffs that are as high as 600 feet among the woods with over 66 miles of trails for hiking. These trails are used for more than just hiking. Visitors use them for horseback riding, bicycling, cross-country skiing, and snowmobiling. Different times of the year bring different events such as summer offers guided walks, tours, art programs, nature, whitewater rafting, swimming in pools, whitewater rafting and hot air ballooning. Winter brings snowmobiling, skiing, and snowboarding.

There is the Humphrey Nature Center that is open all year round and has education sessions for schools, youth groups, and the general public that highlight geology, wildlife, and the parks ecology. There are tent and trailer campsites along with winterized cabins for camping.

BONUS TIP 12. NIAGARA FALLS STATE PARK

This is a waterfall that is along the New York and Canada border. 1,100 feet long and almost 180 feet high, the views are spectacular. The River is used to produce hydroelectric power, which is enough for more than a quarter of New York and Ontario power usage.

Adventure Theater has Niagara: Legends of Adventure, which is a 40 minute presentation of the adventures, myths, and mysteries in the falls.

A few blocks away is the Aquarium of Niagara. There are more than 1,500 animals including California sea lions, Peruvian penguins and more.

Do you like things a little wild? If so, try the Cave of Winds. It is a walk into the stormy mist zone and you will have souvenir sandals and ponchos.

History about Niagara Falls and all the activities that it has can be found in the Discovery Center. It will provide the hiking trails along the park and the specific geographies.

If you like color, check out the falls when the fireworks or illuminations are performed. They are each done on a scheduled basis and show you beauty.

Maid of the Mist is a water adventure. It begins at the Observation Tower and then goes past the base of the American Falls to the Horseshoe Falls.

Ride the Trolley and see all the scenic areas. The fun facts will be presented along with seeing the most popular attractions.

BONUS TIP 13. HUDSON VALLEY

Hudson valley has the world-famous Culinary Institute of America, farm markets, wineries, craft-breweries, food festival legend. It is also known for the Angry Orchard's cider house and custom motorcycles made on American Chopper.

BONUS TIP 14. HUDSON VALLEY PARKS AND RECREATION

Check out the home of the preeminent American artist of the mid-19th century Frederick Edwin Church. It has five miles of road that carriages use and has a gorgeous view of the Hudson valley and Catskills Mountains. There are seasonal programs and events such as birding, snow-shoeing, and cross country skiing. On the lake recreation includes: fishing, kayaking, and other non-motor boats.

BONUS TIP 15. HUDSON VALLEY HISTORY

There are different museums and galleries to check out. FASNY Museum of Firefighting has hands-on interactives and over 60 pieces of apparatus. Franklin D. Roosevelt President Library and Museum has the Great Depression to World War II, Old Rhinebeck Aerodrome Museum & Air Shows has the WWI airplanes, the barnstorming era, and the beginning of aviation.

Hudson Hall is the oldest New York Theater. They have concerts, exhibitions, readings, dances, and more.

BONUS TIP 16. HUDSON VALLEY ENTERTAINMENT

Club Helsinski Hudson is a live-music and art venue for new talent. It brings in thousands of artists throughout the year.

Try the SplashDown Beach and Catskill Animal Sanctuary for the kids. SplashDown Beach is "America's Biggest Little Water Park". There are different water rides, picnic areas, and the Arctic Plunge Mat Racer (five story drag race). The Catskill

Animal Sanctuary has a farm of animals that have been saved or rescued from abuse or neglect. There are tours available and The Homestead has overnight with the pre-Civil war farmhouse setting.

BONUS TIP 17. THOUSAND ISLANDS SEAWAY

It is most well-known for the amount of different locations to see such as state parks for hiking, camping, boating and trophy fishing. However, people don't realize there are also castles, museums, trails, and canyons to visit.

There a many different parks in this area to visit. Each of them has their own uniqueness. All of them are good for picnics and family time, but some have boat rentals, sandy beach areas, campsites and swimming sites.

BONUS TIP 18. THOUSAND ISLANDS SEAWAY HISTORY

Singer Castle on Dark Island was built between 1900 and 1905. It has 28 rooms and was occupied by fifth CEO of Singer Sewing Machine Company

Frederic Bourne. There is a clock tower that is five stories high, four story boat house, squash court, rose garden, hidden passageways into just about all the rooms and outbuildings. A great history attraction that has overnight accommodations.

BONUS TIP 19.   THOUSAND ISLANDS SEAWAY PARKS AND RECREATION

1000 Islands Campground has a family oriented setting. There are hayrides, kids' castle, pirate ship, playground and a wooden tractor on the wagon. There are 44 power hook-up sites and handicap accessible bathrooms.

Two great places to stay are the 1000 Islands Harbor Hotel and the 1000 Islands Wooden Boat Inn. They have luxury accommodations, screened in porches and are located accessible to wine trails, craft breweries, distilleries, lighthouses, and more.

BONUS TIP 20.   LONG ISLAND

Long Island is in the Atlantic Ocean. There ae four counties along this island that runs almost parallel to Connecticut. These counties are Kings, Queens, Nassau, and Suffolk. The entertainment and site seeing would last a lifetime with over 500 places to visit.

BONUS TIP 21. LONG ISLAND ENTERTAINMENT

There are wine regions only minutes from Manhattan.

- Harbes Family Farm & Vineyard with pumpkin picking, corn mazes, hayrides and sweet corn, along with award-winning wines.
- North Fork has almost every style of wine available. There are more than 30 tasting rooms available with gorgeous views and seasonal outside seating. There is:
  o Bedell Cellars
  o Duck Walk Vineyards
  o Lieb Cellars
  o Pindar Vineyards
  o Macari Vineyards

There is the Belmont Park racetrack that opened in 1905. It has two schedules that run from April through mid-July. It has the Belmont Stakes each year which is known as the most difficult 'Triple Crown" to win. There is a free tram ride through the stables, a Paddock show, and a demonstration from Starting Gate.

For kids there is family entertainment that is available both inside and outside.

• Adventureland Amusement Park has more than 30 kids and adult rides available. There is an indoor arcade with prizes to win by redeeming points.

• Deep Hallow Ranch has a history of America's oldest cattle ranch from 1658. They have horseback riding trails, cattle herding with border collies, mares, foals, and more.

• Splish Splash Waterpark is 96 acres of fun with rides and attractions. There is a Lazy River, slides, a section just for kids of the Elephant Slide, Octopus Pool, Monsoon Lagoon, and Pirates Cover. Restaurants and food kiosks are available with lockers and changing rooms.

• Long Island Aquarium contains a 120,000 gallon shark tank! It has sea lion shows, touch tanks, and coral reef displays. There are exhibits with butterflies to bugs. It has been named one of the Top 10 Aquariums for Children.

• Cradle Aviation Museum has over 100 years of Long Islands Aerospace in one location. There is an IMAX Dome Theater, Red Planet Café, and the Reckson Special Events Center.

BONUS TIP 22. LONG ISLAND PARKS AND RECREATION

Jones Beach State Park has a boardwalk, concerts, and areas popular for swimming, biking, trophy fishing, and celebrity sightings.

BONUS TIP 23. LONG ISLAND HISTORY

Oheka Castle is a mansion to see. It is included on the National Register of Historic Places and it is also a member of Historic Hotels in America. It has 32 luxurious guestrooms and suites, is one of the most reputable wedding venues, and offers tours of the gardens and estates.

Old Westbury Gardens a 44-room English manor house that has over 200 acres of formal garden is a beautiful exploration. There are priceless antiques artwork and wooded paths.

There is a lot of sightseeing locations such as the Montauk Lighthouse. It was constructed after George

Washington authorized construction in 1796. It was constructed because there had been so many ships lost on the reefs at land's end.

BONUS TIP 24. NEW YORK CITY

It is known as the capital of world's entertainment. There is so much to see and so many places to go, it is almost impossible to list all of it with details. Therefore, here are the most popular, frequently heard about places to visit, but watch as you're going from one of these sites to another and take in as much as possible. There are over 20,000 restaurants and food stands along the sidewalk that are available and more than you can imagine for stores.

BONUS TIP 25. NEW YORK CITY ENTERTAINMENT

Empire State Building soars 1,454 feet above Manhattan. There is a red carpet VIP guest area, observatories available on the 86th and 102nd floor, and an interactive museum.

Rockefeller Center is a place for skaters. It is known for the annual Christmas tree and the amazing stores that surround it. There are three different observation decks to see the skyline for an unforgettable site.

Yankee Stadium was built in 2009 for the 27-time winning New York Yankees. There is not only Yankee baseball games played there, there are different events hosted such as college football, concerts, and International soccer.

The Bronx Zoo has over 6,000 animals in a 265 acre re-creation of natural habitat. In the colder times of the year there is Tiger Mountain or Himalayan Highlands to visit to see the large cats enjoying the cold and the tropical life can be seen in the World of Reptiles or JungleWorld.

The Staten Island Ferry ride will show the city from a different perspective. The ride is 25 minutes long traveling from Manhattan to Staten Island passing the Statue of Liberty.

Everybody has heard about Central Park and it is hard to picture in your mind a huge recreational area in the middle of a city, let alone New York City. It is definitely a place to visit to grasp the 840 acres of recreational landscaping history. There is entertainment within such as a zoo, sports facilities, theater, lakes, and food.

If you like music, check out Carnegie Hall. They have veterans that perform classical jazz, folk, and more. There are showcases to check out with memorabilia from some of the finest like Judy Garland and the Beatles.

Coney Island & Amusement Park was built in 1920. It has the Cyclone roller coaster, Deno's Wonder Wheel, a circus, sideshows, and a museum. It is a great path of history with the perfect safety record and 150 feet heights on the Coney Island beach to the Manhattan skyline.

Madison Square Garden is known for its legend, iconic athletes, musicians, performers, and even presidents and popes that have been there. It seats 19,500 and more in the state-of-the-art configuration to accommodate special events.

Times Square is a site! There are so many retailers in the huge high buildings to visit. It is known for the flashing neon lights, digital billboards, costumed musicians and characters performing on the street. Everyone knows it because of the ball dropping every New Year's Eve, but to feel it is unbelievable.

BONUS TIP 26. NEW YORK CITY HISTORY

9/11 Memorial & Museum of the World Trade Center Observatory has two reflecting pools to show the footprints of the Twin Towers and the names of the victims and those that risked their lives to save others inscribed in the bronze to ever leave their mark.

One of the most famous historical landmarks is the Statue of Liberty. It was a friendship gift from France with the intention of hope to immigrants as they approached the United States through Ellis Island.

FAMOUS NEW YORK FOOD:

- Manhattan Clam Chowder
- Buffalo Wild Wings
- The Reuben
- The Waldorf Salad
- Eggs Benedict
- Hamburgers
- Hot Dogs

SLANG:: THE NOTORIOUS NYC ACCENT

- Whack = Appalling/Crazy!
- Lit = Amazing/Super cool
- Grill = Staring rudely
- Beef = Having a grudge with another person
- Bridge and Tunnel = Anyone from outside NYC
- Bodega = Convenience/Grocery store
- Waiting on line = Waiting in line/Waiting in a queue
- Cop = Buy or Shop
- Thirsty = Acting desperate
- Mad = Very

ACTIVITIES

Hunting, Fishing, Camping, Skiing, Skating, Amusements parks, Baseball, Boating/Sailing, Mountain Climbing, Historic site seeing, etc. at some the following attractions:

- Statue of Liberty
- Ellis Island
- Times Square
- Niagara Falls
- Central Park
- Finger Lakes
- Lake Placid
- Lake George
- Cooperstown
- Thousand Islands
- The Adirondacks
- Letchworth State Park
- Darwin D. Martin House Complex
- Watkins Glen State Park
- George Eastman House International Museum of Photography and Film

TOP REASONS TO BOOK THIS TRIP

- Enjoy all of New York's nature and what it has to offer in the different seasons
- Learn about New York's history, sports, art, and more
- Visit an assortment of New York's parks from amusement, to water from inland to New York City.

REFERENCES:

AZ Quotes, Mark Twain (1976). "Mark Twain's Notebooks &
Journals, Volume I: (1855-1873)", p.302, Univ of California Press.
Retrieved from: https://www.azquotes.com/quote/830483

14 Top-Rated Tourist Attractions in New York State, by Lana Law
and Lara Seavey. Copyright 2020 PlanetWare Inc.. Retrieved from:
https://www.planetware.com/tourist-attractions/new-york-usny.htm

I Love New York, 2020 New York Department of Economic
Development , Copyright 2020, retrieved from:
https://www.iloveny.com/places-to-go/

Spoiled NYC, Where Else but NYC? 11 Famous Foods That Were
Invented in this Wonderful City, (2015, May 18) Retrieved from:
https://spoilednyc.com/2015/05/18/else-nyc-11-famous-foods-invented-
wonderful-city/

Big Seven Media, 10 New York Slang Words to Sound like A
Local – Big 7 Travel., Copyright 2019. Retrieved from:
https://bigseventravel.com/2019/08/10-new-york-slang-words-to-
sound-like-a-local/

New York Citation Information, History.com, Copyright 2020 from
A&E Television Networks, LLC, Retrieved on May 12, 2020 from:
https://www.history.com/topics/us-states/new-york

Letchworth State Park, Voted Best Attraction in New York State,
(2020) Retrieved on May 12, 2020, from:
https://parks.ny.gov/parks/79/details.aspx

The Adirondack Mountains of Northern New York, Copyright
2002-2020, from I Love New York, on May 12, 2020 from:
https://visitadirondacks.com/

Your Guide to Saratoga Springs, NY, Copyright 2020, Retrieved on
May 13, 2020, from https://www.saratoga.com/

The Catskills, Travel Close, Discover More, Copyright 2020, from I
Love New York, on May 12, 2020 from:
https://www.visitthecatskills.com/

Chautauqua County Visitors Bureau, Play, Laugh, Learn.
Copyright 2020, from Chautauqua County Visitors Bureau, on May 14,
2020, from https://www.tourchautauqua.com/

Peek 'n Peak Resort, Retrieved on May 14, 2020 from:
https://www.pknpk.com/

Ellicottville, We're Still Awesome!!!, Retrieved on May 14, 2020
from: https://www.ellicottvilleny.com/

NY Falls, Lake Erie Parks & Beaches, Copyright 2020
NYFalls.com, Matthew Conheady, Retrieved on May 14, 2020 from:
https://nyfalls.com/lakes/erie/?no_redirect=true

Visit Buffalo Niagara, I Love New York, Retrieved on May 15,
2020 from:
https://www.visitbuffaloniagara.com/?utm_source=madden&utm_medi
um=googlecpc&utm_content=buffalo&utm_campaign=dmnybuff&gcli
d=Cj0KCQjw-
_j1BRDkARIsAJcfmTH7cqFI7Tcl5JXwvT7_I9O3xRr26cD18KRO5S
waLTYkK6yhwXWIXQAaAovQEALw_wcB

Cooperstown, Otsego County, I Love NY, Retrieved on May 15,
2020 from: https://www.thisiscooperstown.com/

15 Places You Absolutely Have To Visit In Binghamton, by Kate
Sherwood, October 23, 2014. Copyright 2020, Binghamton University
State University of New York, Retrieved on May 15, 2020 from.
https://www.binghamton.edu/blog/index.php/blog/story/12545/places-
you-absolutely-have-to-visit-in-binghamton-ny/

City of Binghamton, New York, Retrieved on May 15, 2020, from:
http://www.binghamton-ny.gov/location-geography-historical-brief

Best Things To Do In Utica, New York - Updated 2020, Retrieved
on May 15, 2020, from: https://trip101.com/article/best-things-to-do-
in-utica-new-york

Rome New York, the Copper City, Retrieved on May 15, 2020
from: https://romenewyork.com/

Trip101, Copyright 2020, Retrieved on May 15, 2020 from:
https://trip101.com/article/best-things-to-do-in-rome-ny

20 Best Things to Do in Watkins Glen, New York, by VI Staff on
April 8, 2020. Retrieved on May 16, 2020 from:
https://vacationidea.com/ny/best-things-to-do-in-watkins-glen-ny.html

Visit Rochester, NY Limitless, There's a reason in every season to
visit Rochester. Copyright 2020. Retrieved on May 16, 2020 from:
http://www.visitrochester.com/

Trip Advisor, Things to Do in Elmira. Copyright 2020. Retrived on May 16, 2020 from: https://www.tripadvisor.com/Attractions-g47682-Activities-Elmira_Finger_Lakes_New_York.html

48 hours in Corning, NY, by Erin Faherty, April 17, 2019. Retrieved on May 16, 2020 from: https://www.iloveny.com/blog/post/48-hours-in-corning-ny/

A day in Waterloo: Photo essay of people, places in Upstate NY village, By Kathe Harrington , Updated May 21, 2019; Posted Feb 07, 2017. Retrieved on May 16, 2020 from: https://www.newyorkupstate.com/finger-lakes/2017/02/a_day_in_waterloo_photo_essay_of_people_places_in_upstate_ny_village.html

Finger Lakes Premier Properties, Copyright 2017, Retrieved on May 16, 2020 from: https://www.fingerlakespremierproperties.com/blog/things-to-do-penn-yan-ny/

Niagara Falls State Park, Delaware North Parks and Resorts, Inc. Copyright 2020, Retrieved on May 16, 2020 from: https://www.niagarafallsstatepark.com/

Hudson Valley Attractions, I love NY, Copyright 2020, Retrieved on May 16, 2020 from: https://www.iloveny.com/places-to-go/hudson-valley/attractions/

Discover Long Island New York, I Love NY, copyright 2020. Retrieved on May 16, 2020 from: https://www.discoverlongisland.com/travel-guide/

PACKING AND PLANNING TIPS

A Week before Leaving

- Arrange for someone to take care of pets and water plants.

- Email and Print important Documents.

- Get Visa and vaccines if needed.

- Check for travel warnings.

- Stop mail and newspaper.

- Notify Credit Card companies where you are going.

- Passports and photo identification is up to date.

- Pay bills.

- Copy important items and download travel Apps.

- Start collecting small bills for tips.

- Have post office hold mail while you are away.

- Check weather for the week.

- Car inspected, oil is changed, and tires have the correct pressure.

- Check airline luggage restrictions.

- Download Apps needed for your trip.

Right Before Leaving

- Contact bank and credit cards to tell them your location.

- Clean out refrigerator.

- Empty garbage cans.

- Lock windows.

- Make sure you have the proper identification with you.

- Bring cash for tips.

- Remember travel documents.

- Lock door behind you.

- Remember wallet.

- Unplug items in house and pack chargers.

- Change your thermostat settings.

- Charge electronics, and prepare camera memory cards.

READ OTHER
GREATER THAN A TOURIST
BOOKS

Greater Than a Tourist- Geneva Switzerland: 50 Travel Tips from a Local by Amalia Kartika

Greater Than a Tourist- St. Croix US Birgin Islands USA: 50 Travel Tips from a Local by Tracy Birdsall

Greater Than a Tourist- San Juan Puerto Rico: 50 Travel Tips from a Local by Melissa Tait

Greater Than a Tourist – Lake George Area New York USA: 50 Travel Tips from a Local by Janine Hirschklau

Greater Than a Tourist – Monterey California United States: 50 Travel Tips from a Local by Katie Begley

Greater Than a Tourist – Chanai Crete Greece: 50 Travel Tips from a Local by Dimitra Papagrigoraki

Greater Than a Tourist – The Garden Route Western Cape Province South Africa: 50 Travel Tips from a Local by Li-Anne McGregor van Aardt

Greater Than a Tourist – Sevilla Andalusia Spain: 50 Travel Tips from a Local by Gabi Gazon

Children's Book: *Charlie the Cavalier Travels the World* by Lisa Rusczyk Ed. D.

85

> TOURIST

Follow us on Instagram for beautiful travel images:
http://Instagram.com/GreaterThanATourist

Follow *Greater Than a Tourist* on Amazon.
>Tourist Podcast
>T Website
>T Youtube
>T Facebook
>T Goodreads
>T Amazon
>T Mailing List
>T Pinterest
>T Instagram
>T Twitter
>T SoundCloud
>T LinkedIn
>T Map

> TOURIST

At *Greater Than a Tourist*, we love to share travel tips with you. How did we do? What guidance do you have for how we can give you better advice for your next trip? Please send your feedback to GreaterThanaTourist@gmail.com as we continue to improve the series. We appreciate your constructive feedback. Thank you.

METRIC CONVERSIONS

TEMPERATURE

110° F —   — 40° C
100° F —
90° F —   — 30° C
80° F —
70° F —   — 20° C
60° F —
50° F —   — 10° C
40° F —
32° F —   — 0° C
20° F —
10° F —   — -10° C
0° F —   — -18° C
-10° F —
-20° F —   — -30° C

To convert F to C:

Subtract 32, and then multiply by 5/9 or .5555.

To Convert C to F:

Multiply by 1.8 and then add 32.

32F = 0C

LIQUID VOLUME

To Convert:..................Multiply by
U.S. Gallons to Liters................ 3.8
U.S. Liters to Gallons 26
Imperial Gallons to U.S. Gallons 1.2
Imperial Gallons to Liters....... 4.55
Liters to Imperial Gallons 22
1 Liter = .26 U.S. Gallon
1 U.S. Gallon = 3.8 Liters

DISTANCE

To convert ....Multiply by
Inches to Centimeters 2.54
Centimeters to Inches 39
Feet to Meters...................... .3
Meters to Feet 3.28
Yards to Meters 91
Meters to Yards 1.09
Miles to Kilometers 1.61
Kilometers to Miles............ .62
1 Mile = 1.6 km
1 km = .62 Miles

WEIGHT

1 Ounce = .28 Grams
1 Pound = .4555 Kilograms
1 Gram = .04 Ounce
1 Kilogram = 2.2 Pounds

TRAVEL QUESTIONS

- Do you bring presents home to family or friends after a vacation?

- Do you get motion sick?

- Do you have a favorite billboard?

- Do you know what to do if there is a flat tire?

- Do you like a sun roof open?

- Do you like to eat in the car?

- Do you like to wear sun glasses in the car?

- Do you like toppings on your ice cream?

- Do you use public bathrooms?

- Did you bring a cell phone and does it have power?

- Do you have a form of identification with you?

- Have you ever been pulled over by a cop?

- Have you ever given money to a stranger on a road trip?

- Have you ever taken a road trip with animals?

- Have you ever gone on a vacation alone?

- Have you ever run out of gas?

- If you could move to any place in the world, where would it be?

- If you could travel anywhere in the world, where would you travel?

- If you could travel in any vehicle, which one would it be?

- If you had three things to wish for from a magic genie, what would they be?

- If you have a driver's license, how many times did it take you to pass the test?

- What are you the most afraid of on vacation?

- What do you want to get away from the most when you are on vacation?

- What foods smell bad to you?

- What item do you bring on ever trip with you away from home?

- What makes you sleepy?

- What song would you love to hear on the radio when you're cruising on the highway?

- What travel job would you want the least?

- What will you miss most while you are away from home?

- What is something you always wanted to try?

- What is the best road side attraction that you ever saw?

- What is the farthest distance you ever biked?

- What is the farthest distance you ever walked?

- What is the weirdest thing you needed to buy while on vacation?

- What is your favorite candy?

- What is your favorite color car?

- What is your favorite family vacation?

- What is your favorite food?

- What is your favorite gas station drink or food?

- What is your favorite license plate design?

- What is your favorite restaurant?

- What is your favorite smell?

- What is your favorite song?

- What is your favorite sound that nature makes?

- What is your favorite thing to bring home from a vacation?

- What is your favorite vacation with friends?

- What is your favorite way to relax?

- Where is the farthest place you ever traveled in a car?

- Where is the farthest place you ever went North, South, East and West?

- Where is your favorite place in the world?

- Who is your favorite singer?

- Who taught you how to drive?

- Who will you miss the most while you are away?

- Who if the first person you will contact when you get to your destination?

- Who brought you on your first vacation?

- Who likes to travel the most in your life?

- Would you rather be hot or cold?

- Would you rather drive above, below, or at the speed limited?

- Would you rather drive on a highway or a back road?

- Would you rather go on a train or a boat?

- Would you rather go to the beach or the woods?

TRAVEL BUCKET LIST

1.

2.

3.

4.

5.

6.

7.

8.

9.

10.

NOTES

Printed in Great Britain
by Amazon

84143549R00068